T0129219

Everyday Saints
Faith One Day at a Time
A DAILY DEVOTIONAL

Marcus Bradley
Author of *Full-Time Savior*

WESTBOW
PRESS®
A DIVISION OF THOMAS NELSON
& ZONDERVAN

WestBow Press books may be ordered through booksellers or by contacting:

WestBow Press
A Division of Thomas Nelson & Zondervan
1663 Liberty Drive
Bloomington, IN 47403
www.westbowpress.com
1 (866) 928-1240

All Scripture references are to the New International Version (NIV) unless noted otherwise. NIV quotations are taken from THE HOLY BIBLE, NEW INTERNATIONAL VERSION®, NIV® Copyright © 1973, 1978, 1984, 2011 by Biblica, Inc.® Used by permission. All rights reserved worldwide.

Scriptures marked NCV are taken from the New Century Version®. Copyright © 2005 by Thomas Nelson. Used by permission. All rights reserved.

Scripture quotations marked (NLT) are taken from the Holy Bible, New Living Translation, copyright © 1996, 2004, 2007 by Tyndale House Foundation. Used by permission of Tyndale House Publishers, Inc., Carol Stream, Illinois 60188. All rights reserved.

When I (the author) took the liberty to emphasize certain portions of Scripture, I did it by using ellipses, parentheses, italics, and possibly other various forms of punctuation. I strongly encourage readers to look up all the Bible passages in their perfect form for themselves.

ISBN: 978-1-5127-8945-4 (sc)
ISBN: 978-1-5127-8946-1 (hc)
ISBN: 978-1-5127-8944-7 (e)

Library of Congress Control Number: 2017908069

Print information available on the last page.

WestBow Press rev. date: 5/26/2017

*To Macy, with love I write and with faith
I hope that this devotional will speak to
your heart when you're all grown up.*

My first book, *Full-Time Savior*, was intended for Christians whose religious experience had been quite burdensome and whose concept of Christianity was more about qualifying for salvation than trusting Christ with it, more about complicated doctrine than God's saving grace, more about obeying rules than loving others, more about finding faults than saving souls, and, quite frankly, more about us than Jesus.

As it turns out, the most receptive people to *Full-Time Savior*, generally speaking, have not been those whom I expected. One of these days I will stop predicting what I think God is going to do and whom I think the Holy Spirit is going to stir. After all, Jesus said the Spirit is unpredictable. Like the wind, we do not know where He comes from or where He goes. We do not know when He will do whatever He does. We know He lives inside of Christians, but we don't know how or when He will choose to manifest Himself. We know He gives us different spiritual gifts, but we don't know who will be blessed with what. We know He will make us more like Jesus, but we don't know at what speed or to what extent any given person will change. We know He will teach us through the Word and throughout life, but we don't know exactly how or what He will teach any specific person. At the end of the day, the only thing we know for certain about the methods of the Holy Spirit is that we can expect Him to show up in unexpected ways at unexpected times and, quite possibly, in unexpected places through unexpected people.

As a result of my learning experience with *Full-Time Savior*, I will not guess or expect whom this devotional, *Everyday Saints*, will inspire and touch. I hope it's you. And I hope it's me. I hope it's all the everyday saints out there—those who are sinners, but made perfect by the grace of God through the blood of Jesus Christ.

Although we are very different people with very different lives, the narrative for each of us is effectively the same. Our struggles on earth may vary, but our eternal hope doesn't change. Our individual purposes are unique, but our collective function is one. We are the church of everyday saints. We are simple and broken people who are fixed and made whole at the foot of the cross. That's who I am. That's who you are. And it's who we'll always be.

January 1

Your sins and mistakes do not make you a failure. They confirm your humanness and qualify you for God's grace.

ᘓᘐᗋᣟᣟᑍᗋᘐᘓ

January 2

God loves all versions of you, so there's no advantage to being dishonest with yourself about who you really are.

January 3

How much do you forgive yourself? That amount will be the limit to your forgiveness of others. Don't you wish you could forgive them more? It starts with forgiving yourself more.

⚜

January 4

For those who experience God's grace deep in their hearts, they can't help but become gracious people themselves.

January 5

Grueling attempts at personal renovation can only take you so far. So instead of straining through high-effort spiritual makeovers, immerse yourself in the grace of Christ and hand the reins of your personal transformation over to the Holy Spirit. For it is by grace you are saved through Christ, and it is by grace you are changed through the Spirit. In the same way that you will never regret the choice to let Jesus save you by His grace instead of your works, you will never regret the choice to let the Spirit change you by His power instead of yours.

January 6

I will be made more like Jesus when I quit trying to do it myself.

January 7

> He who began a good work in you will carry it
> on to completion until the day of Christ Jesus.
> (Philippians 1:6)

January 8

It's easier to trust that God has a plan for your future than it is to trust
Him with the path He has in mind to get you there.

January 9

God will never feel compelled to run things by you first. So don't worry about figuring it all out. He'll let you know something when He wants to.

⌘

January 10

God knows the best time to give the promotion. He knows the best time to provide a spouse or a baby. He knows the best time for you to see certain character flaws in yourself. He knows the best time to provide everything.

January 11

Although it seems like we're always waiting on God, sometimes He's just waiting on us.

⁓⧉⁓

January 12

Back when I was a thirty-two year old bachelor, I chose to quit praying and searching for a wife. Instead, I prayed to be a godlier man. I met Amy shortly thereafter.

Make no mistake: I did not suddenly become a great man, nor had I discovered a secret way to pray or anything like that. What I did was try to align myself with God as much as possible. My prayer was no longer for God to serve me and my wishes, but for me to serve Him and His wishes. It was no longer about *receiving* something, but *becoming* something.

January 13

> But seek first his kingdom and his righteousness,
> and all these things will be given to you as well.
> (Matthew 6:33)

January 14

Often times, God blesses us and answers our prayers in ways we don't recognize immediately. But we can be certain that the future holds the gift of hindsight and it will prove that God was faithful all along.

January 15

God is not human, that he should lie, not a human being, that he should change his mind. Does he speak and then not act? Does he promise and not fulfill? (Numbers 23:19)

⚜

January 16

Waiting on God is often deflating, but it's always worth it. As time passes, don't let your hopes and dreams slip away; just set them aside, as necessary, but keep them in the back of your mind. One day you'll know why you did.

"For I know the plans I have for you," declares the Lord, "plans to prosper you and not to harm you, plans to give you hope and a future. Then you will call upon me and come and pray to me, and I will listen to you. You will seek me and find me when you seek me with all your heart." (Jeremiah 29:11–13)

January 18

To move forward with God *never* happens when I demand that He fits into my way of thinking, neatly into my life.

January 19

Embrace the changes of life as an adventure with God. Trust that He knows what He's doing as He alters you on the inside and shuffles your surroundings on the outside.

⚜

January 20

Sometimes doing everything in my power to keep change from happening is doing everything in my power to stop God from moving.

January 21

> Whoever finds their life will lose it, and whoever loses their life for my sake will find it. (Matthew 10:39)

❧

January 22

Choosing earthly security limits spiritual potential.

January 23

Think less about leaving a legacy of your own and more about furthering the legacy of Jesus Christ and His kingdom.

> (Jesus) must become greater; I must become less.
> (John 3:30)

❦

January 24

There are many reasons why people in today's world are absurdly overbusy. Some people are simply greedy, so they devote their lives to money and spend all their time trying to make more of it. Some people just can't say no to anything or anyone, so they drag through life with full plates and empty tanks, surviving on late nights and morning caffeine. Then there are the folks who take pride in their busyness; it's an important part of their identity. Others stay extra busy so they won't have to stop and think about what's really going on in their lives. But perhaps the most common reason to be overly busy is because that's just the world we live in. It's a standard pattern of society. Breakneck speed and bursting schedules are status quo for life in the twenty-first century. And we all seem to fall right in line with that, for one reason or another, as if it's a requirement.

Do not conform to the pattern of this world, but be transformed by the renewing of your mind. Then you will be able to test and approve what God's will is— his good, pleasing and perfect will. (Romans 12:2)

January 26

Developing your spiritual gifts may not be vital for your own salvation, but it could be to someone else's.

January 27

Life does not have to be so busy. There are tough choices to be made in our lives that would help us slow down and find balance. Such balance would allow us to be more useful and available for God, not to mention our families. Regardless of what the world believes (and most employers), you don't have to be stretched so thin that your spiritual life and family life suffer.

What choices could you make to put your life into proper balance? Could you take a less demanding job? What about not tackling the extra projects right now? Do you need to learn how to say no to people who don't live with you, so you can start saying yes to those who do? There is always a way to reduce the madness and slow the whirlwind of life, but you have to be willing to reassess your priorities and let some things go.

January 28

The more important Jesus becomes in your life, the less important earthly things will be. The more you crave eternal things, the looser the grip the temporary things will have on your life. The more you yearn for Christ, the less you will need anything of this earth to give you a sense of value.

January 29

Jesus is the fulfillment of everything. He fulfills the Law, the Prophets, the blood sacrifice to atone for sin, and the hope of eternal life. He also fulfills our longing for love and acceptance. He is all you'll ever need if you let Him be that for you.

January 30

The dream solutions we come up with are often on the surface— money, mood aids, getting married, having a baby, starting an exercise regimen, finding a perfect job, attending the perfect church, fixing the people around me, fixing myself... But none of those things are the solution. Jesus is the solution.

The unconditional love of Christ accepts you for who you are right now. Jesus doesn't love you just because you have some good qualities or potential. He doesn't gloss over your bad stuff to cherry-pick the good. He doesn't ignore your weaknesses; *He loves you in spite of them.* Jesus loves you with up-to-the-minute, present-day, no-matter-what love. That's what makes it unconditional. And that's what makes it real.

The heart of Christ exposed is infinitely more powerful than perfectly articulated, intellectual words.

February 2

To love God, to love our spouses, and to love each other is a commitment, not an emotion. We are to commit ourselves to loving God and each other with the *everlasting* love of God instead of the roller-coaster love of human emotion. Emotional love is unsustainable and often hinges on circumstance or mood, but everlasting love is an irrevocable pledge of allegiance. God's love is a covenant to you that cannot be undone, and we are expected to pursue a heart that can love like that.

February 3

Aiming for love is reaching for God, because "God is love" (1 John 4:8).

Love is not calculating. Love does not manipulate others or make them feel guilty. Love does not deceive or operate with secret motives. Love is honest. Love forgives. Love waits. Love has no reason to scheme or control, because it trusts God to do what is right.

February 5

The Lord is the Spirit, and where the Spirit of the Lord is, there is freedom. And we ... are being transformed into his image with ever-increasing glory, which comes from the Lord, who is the Spirit. (2 Corinthians 3:17–18)

February 6

Anyone who knew me twenty years ago would agree that I needed more grace than most. Now that my life has dramatically turned around, such that I no longer resemble the man of my past, I can confidently say that I need just as much grace now as I did then.

We will always need grace.

⸎

February 7

It's funny how we forget about grace as we jockey ourselves to be in position for it. But there are no positions for grace. We are incapable of getting ourselves in line for salvation. That's why Jesus came to die on the cross for us. And we can't change that. We'll never escape our need for grace.

February 8

The fear of being a disappointment or a failure is not an excuse for perfectionism. It's a symptom of it. The disease of perfectionism requires two things:

1. An infatuation with faults;
2. A constant focus on self.

Those two traits are a combustible combination that often leads to self-righteousness on the good days and self-pity on the bad ones. Either way, perfectionism guarantees unhealthy perceptions and relationships, and it just might cause you to miss the point of the cross.

February 9

There's nothing more important in your Christian walk than letting go of all regrets and forgiving yourself completely.

February 10

Trusting Jesus for salvation does not insinuate that He will help you become more deserving of it. It means your undeserving-ness doesn't matter!

⚜

February 11

A burglar drives by thousands of houses without robbing one. A gossip can go weeks without spreading negativity. A liar can tell the whole truth some of the time. But it only takes one slip-up to be guilty. It only takes one blunder to deserve jail, hell, or shunning of some kind. But fortunately, it only takes one cross to wipe every single one of our sins away.

People cannot do any work that will make them right with God. So they must trust in Him, who makes even evil people right in His sight. Then God accepts their faith, and that makes them right with Him. (Romans 4:5 NCV)

The spiritually mature can care less about being spiritually mature; they just are. They don't pat themselves on the back for their spiritual prowess; they just live with gratitude. They don't need to know why everything is the way it is; they just move forward in faith every day. They don't need to figure God out; they just trust Him.

February 14

> The Lord foils the plans of the nations; he thwarts the purposes of the peoples. But the plans of the Lord stand firm forever; the purposes of his heart through all generations. Blessed is the nation whose God is the Lord. (Psalm 33:10–12)

February 15

The key to a fulfilling life—in a practical sense—is to want what you have, not what you don't.

> Be thankful in all circumstances, for this is God's will
> for you who belong to Christ Jesus. (1 Thessalonians
> 5:18 NLT)

When we begin a Bible study with a conclusion already in mind, the findings will be skewed. Anyone can find a few passages to take out of context and justify a selfish cause. But the Word is living and active; it will penetrate your very soul if you allow it (Hebrews 4:12). So I urge you to give God the opportunity to speak to your heart every time you open the Bible. Let Him show you what He wants you to see. No agendas. No preconceived notions. Just an honest and open heart that is willing to yield to the Spirit.

February 18

> Do not worry about your life ... Who of you by
> worrying can add a single hour to his life? ... Therefore
> do not worry about tomorrow, for tomorrow will
> worry about itself. Each day has enough trouble of
> its own. (Matthew 6:25–27, 34)

February 19

Don't miss the joys of life today by being so busy working toward and
wondering about tomorrow.

February 20

If you make $40,000 a year, live within your means. If you make $100,000, live like you make forty.

⁂

February 21

Notice the similarities between the words "discipline" and "disciple." When we are willing to live a disciplined lifestyle, it's easier for God to mold us into His disciples.

February 22

One important signature of discipline is being able to say no, even to some things that may seem good. Too many "good" things will weigh you down, compromise your mission, and keep you from your purpose.

❧

February 23

There's a fine line between *availability* and *vulnerability*—know the difference. Stay alert. Be disciplined. Know your limitations and don't overdo it. The disciplined and well-rested version of you is best for *everyone* in the long run, even those who demand the most of you, whether that's your employer, your family, your church family, or even yourself. Don't ignore your physical and spiritual well-being in order to meet relentless expectations.

If you drill down deep, behind all the reasons for our high divorce rates, you will find that the busyness of today's world is a key contributor. Make it a priority to slow down. Grow together as people. Take the time to mature in love and faith. Your professions, bank accounts, and social appearances aren't as important as you. And your kids need you too. They will grow up watching you determine what's important in life. Is it careers, nice stuff, and social activities, or is it love? Is it each other, or is it everyone and everything else? Is it religion and church duties, or is it growing deeper with Jesus? What do you want out of life? What is important to you? Your lifestyle reveals your answer. Your lifestyle reveals your heart.

February 25

Your life—mind, body, and soul—will reflect what you do in your spare time. And if you have no spare time, then that will be evident in your reflection: Hectic. Frantic. Frazzled. Chaotic. Running late. Short fuse.

Make some spare time. It's a vital commodity for your quality of life. Then use that time for yourself, the people closest to you, and your Savior. Spare time used wisely pays immediate dividends for you and your family, and it makes *eternal impact* on future generations.

February 26

All of our idols are revealed by stepping back and analyzing what's keeping us so busy.

⁂

February 27

Jesus knows what you struggle with. He knows the junk in your life, but He doesn't care. He was crucified for you *because* of that junk. In fact, He saw your sins take the form of nails, and He allowed them to be driven into His flesh. He knew it was for you, and that's why He did it—because He loves you.

February 28

Nothing in this world is more important to God than you.

⚜

February 29

You are exactly who God had in mind when He created you. You are not a mistake, but the result of a brilliant plan. God made you who you are on purpose. You are hand-crafted and well-made, just like the rest of His creation.

> God saw all that He had made, and it was very good. (Genesis 1:31)

> I praise You because I am fearfully and wonderfully made; Your works are wonderful, I know that full well. (Psalm 139:14)

> I am the vine; you are the branches. If you remain
> in me and I in you, you will bear much fruit. (John
> 15:5)

Although we are guaranteed to produce fruit if we abide in Jesus, we are not guaranteed to see it. So don't be discouraged if you don't currently see any fruit with your own eyes. If you remain glued to Christ, you will produce fruit.

March 2

In order for a tree to maximize its fruit production it gets pruned. Webster's definition of pruning is "to cut off or cut back parts of for better shape or more fruitful growth." Basically, pruning redirects the growth pattern of a tree (and cuts off the dead spots) so it can become more fruitful.

John 15:2 says that God will prune you. He will cut off parts of you and reshape you. As you probably already know, the process of pruning does not feel good. It is quite painful when God redirects you and forces you to change and die to self. But just remember, God's redirection is not a form of rejection; it is an honor. God is pruning you because He has plans for you to be more fruitful.

March 3

God made you with a specific intention in mind. There's a reason for you.

⊂⊸⊰⊱⊷⊃

March 4

Only God knows the heart (1 Kings 8:39) and only God's heart is good (Mark 10:18); but perhaps a strong desire for a pure heart is pure in itself, and as pure a human heart can be. Wanting a pure heart is taking a step in God's direction, and it certainly gives Him something to work with.

Do you want a pure heart? What *are* your desires? What do you strive for? What do you love? What do you think about? What does God see when He examines your heart?

March 5

The crucible for silver and the furnace for gold, but
the Lord tests the heart. (Proverbs 17:3)

March 6

Repentance is a commitment to getting back on track, not beating
yourself up for getting off track.

March 7

Forgiveness understands failure. It interprets failure as a temporary lapse on the way to achieving the ultimate goal. If you keep trying, then each failure is one step closer to getting it right. The only failure is to stop trying.

⚜

March 8

> Let no debt remain outstanding, except the continuing debt to love one another, for whoever loves others has fulfilled the law. The commandments, "You shall not commit adultery," "You shall not murder," "You shall not steal," "You shall not covet," and whatever other command there may be, are summed up in this one command: "Love your neighbor as yourself." (Romans 13:8–9)

March 9

If the only way I know how to love myself is if I am perfect, then the only way I'll be able to love others is if they are perfect.

⸞⸞⸞

March 10

To be righteous does not mean to be good enough. Nor does it mean to live right or do right, and it certainly doesn't mean to *be* right. It means to be *made* right. And we are made right in God's sight by faith in Jesus Christ.

> We are made right with God by placing our faith in Jesus Christ. And this is true for everyone who believes, no matter who we are. (Romans 3:22 NLT)

The ultimate pride is to believe that being made right with God has something to do with you.

> He saved us, not because of righteous things we had done, but because of His mercy. (Titus 3:5)

> Pride leads to disgrace, but with humility comes wisdom. (Proverbs 11:2 NLT)

March 13

By definition, the only way to be humble is to not know that you are. If you truly seek God, He will help you develop humility without you knowing it.

⚜

March 14

If I cared to dissect, I would probably find that there's not a church out there that sees everything exactly as I do. But I have zero desire to put churches under a microscope to look for things to disagree with. If I required perfection from a church, I would never go to one. More importantly, if God required perfection from our churches, He'd spend eternity alone. The point is this: Since God doesn't expect a church to be perfect, we shouldn't either. Always remember that we are imperfect humans who attend imperfect churches to worship the perfect God.

March 15

No matter how hard I try, I will never be a spiritual superstar. That's because God chose me to live on earth as a human.

⁓⊙⧟⊙⁓

March 16

Knowledge is good, but to *pursue* it can cross a line. In fact, it was the pursuit of knowledge and the lure of its power that led to the downfall of the entire human race (Genesis 2:16–3:24). Eve introduced sin to the world because she couldn't resist the idea that knowledge could glorify her. The truth is we haven't changed very much since then. Thousands of years later, we still imply glorification when we say things like, "knowledge is power." But we can't forget where we came from. We cannot sidestep the truth: it was the quest for knowledge that gave birth to our sins. Therefore, as we grow in religious knowledge, perhaps the most important thing to learn is to learn what's really important:

> While knowledge makes us feel important, it is love that strengthens the church. (1 Corinthians 8:1 NLT)

Supplement your faith with a generous provision of moral excellence, and moral excellence with knowledge, and knowledge with self-control, and self-control with patient endurance, and patient endurance with godliness, and godliness with brotherly affection, and brotherly affection with love for everyone. The more you grow *like this*, the more productive and useful you will be in your knowledge of our Lord Jesus Christ. (2 Peter 1:5–8 NLT)

March 18

We only have partial knowledge, and even that knowledge passes away (1 Corinthians 13:8–9). Knowledge is weak and fleeting, but love lasts forever (Psalm 106:1; 1 Corinthians 13:8). Paul said that only three things will endure forever—faith, hope, and love—and the greatest of these is love (1 Corinthians 13:13).

March 19

Heart-based obedience is different than head-based. For example, following orders is not necessarily a function of love; so it's very possible to outwardly obey God without inward love for Him (Matthew 23:23–28). Therefore, obedience alone does not prove love. It *could* be love, but it could also be self-preservation (out of fear) or self-righteousness (out of pride).

So how do we know whether our obedience to God is love-based? The Bible says our love for each other proves us to be authentic disciples and spiritually alive (John 13:35; 1 John 3:14; 4:7–12). Genuine love for one another is not the result of a rule, a sermon, or a book page; it's the result of a heart change that can only come from the Holy Spirit. Heart changes occur with progression in the lives of those who love God and yield to His Spirit for the re-shaping of self into the image of Christ.

March 20

> We ought always to thank God for you, brothers and sisters, and rightly so, because your faith is growing more and more, and the love all of you have for one another is increasing. (2 Thessalonians 1:3)

Christians from other styles and denominations are your teammates who play a different position than you, not competitors from another team.

> I appeal to you, dear brothers and sisters, by the authority of our Lord Jesus Christ, to live in harmony with each other. Let there be no divisions in the church. Rather, be of one mind, united in thought and purpose. (1 Corinthians 1:10 NLT)

March 23

Differing vision equals *division.*

⚜

March 24

Some clumping of like-minded believers will occur (thus our separate church brands), but no *divisions* should occur. No steamy debates with your brethren who serve the same Jesus as you.

March 25

God accepts our differences. In fact, He created them.

⚜

March 26

We are not called to be replicas. There is no perfect way for a person to be. There is no perfect path for a person to take. No perfect family to emulate. No perfect church to attend. There is not even a perfect interpretation of the Bible, even though the Bible itself is perfect. For us, our only hope is in the perfect Savior. And through His blood, He makes each of us uniquely perfect in God's eyes, independent of anyone and everyone else.

March 27

God delights in the details of you. He loves the little things you do. He cares about the same things as you, even the miniscule. He pays attention and chuckles along with you. After all, He made you for His enjoyment and His glory.

❦

March 28

If the good outweighs the bad, why focus on the bad? And if the bad outweighs the good, let the Holy Spirit transform your mind to think positively.

Finally, brothers and sisters, whatever is true, whatever is noble, whatever is right, whatever is pure, whatever is lovely, whatever is admirable—if anything is excellent or praiseworthy—think about such things. (Philippians 4:8)

⚜

March 30

Jesus loves you so much that He determined it was worth it to die for you. And that kind of love affects you. I don't care who you are. If you let that reach your heart, you will be changed.

We love others because our hearts have softened with the love of the Lord, and we want everyone else to know this love of God and this God of love.

⌒⌒⌒✿⌒⌒⌒

Here is a trustworthy saying that deserves full acceptance: Christ Jesus came into the world to save sinners—of whom I am the worst. But for that very reason I was shown mercy so that in me, the worst of sinners, Christ Jesus might display His immense patience as an example for those who would believe in Him and receive eternal life. (1 Timothy 1:15–16)

April 2

If you were the only person on earth, Jesus Christ would still carry that cross up to Calvary and be crucified.

⚜

April 3

Holy living is not a requirement for salvation, but rather a love response to the One who has freed us of all requirements.

April 4

Live as free people, but do not use your freedom as an excuse to do evil. Live as servants of God. (1 Peter 2:16 NCV)

April 5

If grace gets one excited to go out and live according to his sinful nature, then he's not living in the Spirit.

April 6

Be as holy as you can be—not for brownie points with God or status in the church, but because that's who you are. God wants your heart. He wants your soul. He wants the inside.

⁂

April 7

We cannot love God simply because we know that we should. We don't *decide* to love Him. We love Him because He first loved us (1 John 4:19). This means that as we experience His love for us, our hearts will respond with more love for Him. And once your heart begins to change, love no longer feels like something you're supposed to do; it becomes who you are.

April 8

Christians are obedient because we want to be, not because we have to be. It's a desire out of gratitude, not a burden to fulfill. It's a disposition, not a set of teachings. It's a way of life, not a list of rules. It's a matter of the heart, not of outward appearance. It's a reflection of the Spirit, not a requirement of the flesh. It's a faith in Jesus, not in self.

April 9

Heart change is evidence of Christ's residence in you.

April 10

Analyzing yourself to death is not very healthy. Some introspection and self-analysis is good, but not in excess; because no matter which angle you take to judge yourself or what lengths you go to improve yourself, the forgiveness of your sins through Jesus Christ is still your only hope.

☙❦❧

April 11

Generally speaking, if you've had big problems in life, then you have big potential for Christ. I am not saying that you *need* huge problems to have potential. That would be an absurd statement. But if your life is, or has been, full of troubles, then your future is packed with potential—because you have a story to tell, lives to touch, and people to affect by what you've overcome. God specializes in converting weaknesses into strengths, turning bad into good, and using lost causes as powerful vessels for Him.

I have chosen you and have not rejected you. So do not fear, for I am with you; do not be dismayed, for I am your God. I will strengthen you and help you; I will uphold you with my righteous right hand. (Isaiah 41:9–10)

April 13

Rule of thumb—when something bad happens, worry about taking care of it. Until then, there's nothing to worry about.

April 14

It is not good to run from problems, but it's worse to focus on them. And to dwell on *potential* problems is what creates 90 percent of them. To fixate on what *could* go wrong ensures that life is always a crisis. Problem-solvers don't look for things to fix; problem-makers do. Be a problem-solver when problems arise in life, not a problem-maker to ensure they do.

April 15

It is a choice whether to be positive or negative. It may not come as naturally for some as it does for others to be positive; but at the end of the day, everyone gets to choose.

> Don't judge others, or you will be judged. You will be judged in the same way that you judge others, and the amount you give to others will be given to you. Why do you notice the little piece of dust in your friend's eye, but you don't notice the big piece of wood in your own eye? (Matthew 7:1–3 NCV)

There is an obvious message in that passage not to judge others for their wrongdoing, because we all have issues. But there's another important truth that the Holy Spirit has taught me from that Scripture:

> Don't accuse others of judging you. If you make such accusations, then you should realize that you are, in fact, in those moments, judging them.

Love does not select the most deserving. Worthiness does not register because none of us are. I am called to love the unworthy, including myself. Especially myself. And, as difficult as it may be, I am even called to love those who think they are worthy.

April 18

Don't focus on whether others love you; instead, make sure to be a model of love for them.

> Love is patient, love is kind. It does not envy, it does not boast, it is not proud. It does not dishonor others, it is not self-seeking, it is not easily angered, it keeps no record of wrongs. Love does not delight in evil but rejoices with the truth. It always protects, always trusts, always hopes, always perseveres. Love never fails. (1 Corinthians 13:4–8)

April 19

If you don't understand God's unconditional love for you, then you could mistakenly interpret His methods of correction as being rejection. But God is not rejecting you:

> My son, do not make light of the Lord's discipline, and do not lose heart when He rebukes you, because the Lord disciplines everyone He loves. (Hebrews 12:5–6)

April 20

If it's commonplace for you to beat yourself up for your own blemishes, then it will likely become just as common for you to rip others to shreds to make yourself feel better.

❦

April 21

If you expect personal perfection, then you'll expect it from others too. That's why perfectionism and healthy relationships never co-exist; because when you look for perfection, you'll always find something to criticize.

Pure honesty assesses who you really are, what your situation really is, and the intentions of your heart. Dishonesty, on the other hand, refuses to see reality or admit the whole truth. Dishonesty prefers a blindfold as it lounges by the lazy pool of partial truths and convenient compromises. The water of deceit feels nice and relaxing as you dip your feet in, but you can't see the crocodiles lurking beneath the surface.

Are you turning a blind eye to the crocodiles in your life? Are you ignoring unwise relationships, sinful behavior, Spiritless legalism, or any other forms of deceit? These are very real crocodiles that will eventually devour you if you don't deal with them. Tiptoeing around the truth doesn't change it. Dancing around dishonesty doesn't diminish it. Trying to justify your convenient compromises doesn't make them okay. At the very point that you get *completely* honest with God, He will make Himself known and show you exactly what you need to do. Pure honesty opens your eyes and shows you the way. And if you follow through with the truth, you will be tremendously blessed.

A light shines in the dark for honest people. (Psalm 112:4 NCV)

April 24

For the last fifteen years or so, I've kept a journal in which I talk to God about life. It's evolved over time—I no longer do it every day, for instance—but it has consistently been a catalyst for personal growth and a benefit to my spiritual life. Whether I'm jotting down my praises and counting my blessings, venting my emotions, or bouncing ideas around, I've found it to be a positive exercise to articulate to God whatever is going on in life. It has certainly strengthened my relationship with Him. Would this be a good idea for you?

April 25

> Those who guard their lips preserve their lives, but those who speak rashly will come to ruin. (Proverbs 13:3)

April 26

One voluntary compliment is worth more than a thousand prompted ones.

⁂

April 27

People like good people. A good name represents Christ well. And that's our job—to represent Jesus. We are to carry out His mission of winning the lost, and a big part of that is achieved by being a good person and caring about others. The truth is nobody will care about what you have to say unless they know you care about what they have to say. They won't be interested unless you are. So go win the lost—start with a caring heart, a listening ear, and a loving attitude.

> Make the teaching about God our Savior attractive
> in every way. (Titus 2:10 NLT)

April 28

The less I speak, the more I will be heard.

⚜

April 29

Good people will always be remembered. They won't be afraid of bad news; their hearts are steady because they trust in the Lord. They are confident and will not be afraid. (Psalm 112:6–8 NCV)

April 30

God will sort things out as we go. Our job is to keep going.

⁂

May 1

> For God is not unjust. He will not forget how hard you have worked for him and how you have shown your love to him by caring for other believers, as you still do. Our great desire is that you will keep on loving others as long as life lasts, in order to make certain that what you hope for will come true. (Hebrews 6:10–11 NLT)

May 2

To wait for God is to wait as long as it takes.

❧❧❧

May 3

When is it time to take a step of faith? When God tells you to. God speaks to each one of us in different ways—the Bible, life circumstances, maybe receiving a word from His Spirit while praying, or some other way. Whatever it is, you must be certain it's God before you act on a whim.

May 4

Some people can't wait any longer, so they force things to happen and label it a faith-move. But to live by faith always requires waiting for God. The longer you wait, the clearer things become. And the clearer things become before you act, the better life gets.

❧

May 5

Sometimes we try to rationalize whatever it is that we *want* God to say as being from Him. But what we believe God is saying has to be real, not manufactured. It must be divine, not simply desired. The aspiration to live by faith can cause us to see a mirage. We want something to be God's will so badly that we find a way to make it seem like it is. We convince ourselves it must be God. But waiting on Him—for His calling in His timing—is absolutely critical to have what it takes to live by faith. If you don't know in the deepest parts of your heart that God is the one telling you to step out in faith, then you probably shouldn't do it. Until you know how God communicates with you, and until you know it is Him in any given instance, don't act on your own. If you aren't sure, just wait a little longer. It will become obvious. In fact, often times, He will eventually force the issue.

May 6

Only you can understand the dreams God has placed in your heart. No one else can understand, nor do they need to. They are *your* dreams.

CRORGRO

May 7

There is a difference between giving up on your dream and putting it on hold. The former is bad for your soul; the latter is often necessary. Sometimes you know why to delay the dream and sometimes you don't. But you can't force your dream if it's not time for it.

There are usually three factors in delayed dreams:

+ You need to tweak it. God will show you the tweaks in His time.
+ You need to learn some things before you're ready for your dream to be realized.
+ You need to wait for others to be in the right positions as well. God has billions of people to maneuver into proper position before it's time for your dream to unfold. So hang in there and commit yourself to growing in the love of God while you wait on Him.

May 8

To hope in God is to believe that He has good things in store for you. To have faith in God is to know that He has your best interests at heart. To love God is to hope that you have His best interests at heart.

⁓

May 9

Godliness with contentment is great gain. For we brought nothing into the world, and we can take nothing out of it. But if we have food and clothing, we will be content with that. People who want to get rich fall into temptation ... For the love of money is a root of all kinds of evil ... But you, man of God, *flee* from all this, and pursue righteousness, godliness, faith, love, endurance and gentleness. (1Timothy 6:6–11)

If you take the time to read the Parable of the Sower in Luke chapter eight, you will see the different scenarios of what can happen when we receive the seed of the Word. Some people let the troubles of life overcome their faith, some harden completely, and others retain the Word in their heart and produce a crop. But I want to focus on the seed that falls among the thorns. The thorns represent the deceitfulness of wealth and cares of this world, which, in the parable, chokes out the plants and keeps them from bearing fruit. Many Christians fall into this category. They care too much about money—or other things of this world—and do not mature in the faith or produce fruit for the Lord (Luke 8:14). They may not be lost, so to speak, but they aren't fruitful. If we want to become fruitful, we cannot allow ourselves to be overtaken by the cares, patterns, and fears of our society. And we certainly cannot become blinded by the dollar.

May 11

> No servant can serve two masters. Either he will hate the one and love the other, or he will be devoted to the one and despise the other. You *cannot* serve both God and Money. (Luke 16:13)

It's easy to believe all "sound" advice, even if it's not from God. Here's how to gauge the advice you receive:

> *Flesh advice* will always revolve around earthly success, outward appearance, money, and achievement.
>
> *Spirit advice* will center on wise relationships, spiritual health and growth, and God's will.

May 13

> If the whole body were an eye, where would the sense of hearing be? If the whole body were an ear, where would the sense of smell be? But in fact God has placed the parts in the body, every one of them, just as he wanted them to be. If they were all one part, where would the body be? As it is, there are many parts, but one body... Now you are the body of Christ, and each one of you is a part of it. (1 Corinthians 12:17–27)

May 14

All Christians are fellow members in the body of Christ. All who serve Jesus—regardless of denomination—are brothers and sisters (or perhaps distant cousins) in the family of God.

May 15

People whose confidence comes from Jesus don't feel the need to compare themselves to others.

May 16

When you study God's Word, do it to learn about Jesus and become more like Him, or do it for fun, but don't do it to poke holes in the beliefs of other Christians. In your daily pursuit of Christ, try to set aside all comparisons, competitions, and agendas. Make it all about Jesus. Make it *honestly* about Jesus.

⚜

May 17

Leave your religious details tucked away in the cabinet of personal curiosity with its contents hidden behind a closed door. The centerpiece of your house is Jesus Christ. You only need to open the cabinets every once in a while.

May 18

Strict religion evolves until the rules become its savior. But the true Savior will always be Jesus. Be wary of the rule-worshippers. Many of them say:

"Yes, Jesus saves, but..."

No! There are no buts! Jesus saves—no ifs, ands, or buts about it.

⚜

May 19

Which do you think God wants more: your love or your perfectly accurate doctrine? I'll tell you what He's not interested in: for you to fall in love with your own perfect accuracy.

May 20

When people know the love of God on an intimate level, they don't constantly seek human approval, nor are they eager to voice their disapproval.

❧

May 21

> Be wise in the way you act toward outsiders; make the most of every opportunity. Let your conversation be always full of grace, seasoned with salt, so that you may know how to answer everyone. (Colossians 4:5–6)

May 22

Try to keep God's love above know-how and God's wisdom above feel-good.

❦

May 23

For the knowledge-seeker, when you comprehend grace, your heart melts and softens as you're taken by the hand down the path of *balanced* truth. You'll see that grace is a manifestation of God's love, and it serves as an anchor for you as you gain knowledge, keeping you from drifting into loveless religion, pointless pursuits of perfection, or graceless salvation.

For those who lean toward the emotional aspect of the faith, the Holy Spirit will teach you to seek God in spirit *and* truth. The grace of God will continue to minister to the emotional needs of your heart, but it will also take you to the Bible, which acts as a stabilizing force of truth as you continue to grow.

May 24

In the end, isn't salvation all that matters? And isn't it comforting to know that your salvation doesn't depend on who you are as much as whom God is? What you do isn't nearly as important as what Jesus did. In fact, *what you do* is entirely inconsequential. *Who you become* is your response to Jesus through the Holy Spirit.

May 25

Jesus is always your Savior. He's not going to leave you in your down times. He's not going to abandon you in your weak times. There's no reason to fear this kind of rejection from Jesus.

> If we are faithless, he remains faithful, for he cannot disown himself. (2 Timothy 2:13)

May 26

Righteousness is not about you. It's not something you can do for yourself. It's not a character trait you can develop. Righteousness is only attained through faith in Jesus Christ.

> There is only one God, and he makes people right with himself only by faith, whether they are Jews or Gentiles. (Romans 3:30 NLT)

May 27

See everyone for who they are, not for who you want them to be or expect them to be, including yourself.

May 28

Holiness does not come from us, and everyday saints are okay with that—in fact, they learn to embrace it with absolute gratitude. They are thrilled that salvation and righteousness come freely through Jesus Christ. And they are able to comprehend the truth that through Christ they are as perfect as anyone has ever been. Thus, the title, *Everyday Saints*—common people full of imperfection, yet perfect people before God.

May 29

Self-righteousness is an attempt to take the place of Christ and be your own savior.

May 30

Perfect standards naturally make you seem more like Christ, but trying to achieve them on your own actually shuts Him out.

⟡⟡⟡⟡⟡⟡

May 31

It seems quite difficult to grasp that faith in someone else—Jesus—*completely* justifies us. So we make it more complicated than it is by throwing in some extra personal responsibility. But it isn't that complicated: only Jesus saves because He is the unblemished Lamb of God. He is the required sacrifice, once for all. And if we believe that the blood of the Lamb pays for our sins, then it's as if we provided a lamb ourselves. Our lamb is to have faith in God's Lamb.

June 1

Let us look only to Jesus, the One who began our faith and who makes it perfect. (Hebrews 12:2 NCV)

❧

June 2

In the gospel of Luke, Jesus rebuked Martha for being "upset over all these details" (Luke 10:41 NLT). In the passage, Martha was frustrated with Mary because Mary wasn't doing the work that needed done. Instead, Mary was busy spending time with Jesus. But as far as Martha was concerned, Mary was neglecting the details of duty. She wasn't paying attention to the things they were supposed to be doing. But Jesus made it very clear to Martha that Mary had discovered what was *actually* important—Him! And it's the same for us—the stuff we're supposed to do doesn't really matter. Jesus is what matters.

June 3

Satan knows the Scriptures better than any of us, but his Scripture knowledge doesn't save him. Knowing the Bible doesn't save us either. Letting the Bible take us to Jesus does (John 5:39–40).

❧

June 4

> If you are trying to make yourselves right with God by keeping the law, you have been cut off from Christ! You have fallen away from God's grace. But we who live by the Spirit eagerly wait to receive *by faith* the righteousness God has promised to us. For when we place our faith in Christ Jesus, there is no benefit in (rules and customs). What is important is faith expressing itself in love. (Galatians 5:4–6 NLT)

June 5

Seeking Jesus will lead you to a life of obedience to God, but seeking a life of obedience may not lead you to Jesus. Just seek Christ with all your being. He's your Savior. He's all you need. Follow *Him* and you will not be led astray.

⁂

June 6

You will experience the perfection of heaven if Jesus Christ is your Savior. You will see the days of no sickness, weakness, and injustice. You will lock arms with the saints of old; and you might be surprised to discover that Peter, John, and all the other saints were just as human as you. They had the same weaknesses you have. And their great hope was the same as yours—Jesus Christ.

June 7

Do you think the disciples of Jesus were strictly business? I don't. I think they were best friends. I think they talked about fishing sometimes. And their families. And the weather. Evidence of their "normalcy" is recorded throughout the Gospels. These men of God were common people, but they had extraordinary experiences with Christ and a story to tell for those who would listen. Yes, it is true that they courageously uprooted their lives for the cause of Christ, but they were still ordinary people like us—they had bills to pay, mouths to feed, and sinful natures to overcome. Think about that: the disciples were no different than you, yet God used them to change the world. Indeed, it's *always* someone like you that God chooses to change the world.

June 8

Without a little eccentricity and extremeness, nothing great gets accomplished. But, often times, with too much eccentricity and extremeness, nothing much gets accomplished at all.

June 9

Which comes first—the end of isolation or the end of self-fixation? Good question. One thing is certain—we need to get our minds off of ourselves. We need to ponder Jesus, think of others, and get out there and let His light shine.

⁂

June 10

No one is above grace and no one is beneath it.

June 11

It may not seem fair if someone less deserving gets into heaven, but it's really not fair that anyone does.

 ❧

June 12

If I think I'm spiritually mature, then I've still got a ways to go.

June 13

My heart is not proud, Lord, my eyes are not haughty;
I do not concern myself with great matters or things
too wonderful for me. But I have stilled and quieted
my soul ... Put your hope in the Lord both now and
forevermore. (Psalm 131:1–3)

June 14

I believe you can simultaneously define humility and spiritual
maturity as the recognition, acceptance, and appreciation of the fact
that God doesn't need anything from you.

June 15

If your seven-year old child was to find a stash of your cash and set it on fire, it would not be his responsibility to go out and earn the money back. The money is gone and it's up to you to make up for it. As God's children, we don't have to pay anything back either.

∽⊰⊱∾

June 16

> It is true that some preach Christ out of envy and rivalry, but others out of goodwill. The latter do so out of love ... The former preach Christ out of selfish ambition, not sincerely ... But what does it matter? The important thing is that in every way, whether from false motives or true, Christ is preached. And because of this I rejoice. (Philippians 1:15–18)

June 17

Jesus is not some tool or medium to use for your entrance into heaven. He is not a stepping stone for advancement in your spiritual journey. He is the ultimate goal, the final destination, and the grand prize. He is your target—the Alpha, the Omega, the Beginning and the End. Jesus is God.

⁘⁘⁘

June 18

Jesus Christ is your full-time Savior. That means He's better than your best and He covers up your worst. It's the substitution effect—He takes your place. He represents you all the time (Hebrews 7:24–27). Therefore, your most awful deeds don't condemn you and your finest ones don't save you. You are His responsibility now, in the good times and the bad.

June 19

The road to spiritual freedom cannot be found when we try to pave it ourselves.

〰️

June 20

A competitive Christian naturally wants to earn the salvation and victory that is freely given to us. And that's the burden that many Christians feel—we try to earn grace. We feel like we should owe something for it. But if that were the case, then it wouldn't be grace (Romans 11:6).

June 21

Your spiritual life becomes weightless when you admit that you need Jesus—not only to save you, but also to transform you.

 ~ ❦ ~

June 22

Spiritual freedom does not necessarily mean "to free" as in "to grant permission." A more accurate description would be "to liberate, as a slave" or "to make it easier, less straining" or "to unhook the chain."

June 23

When half your life is spent fearing your own sins and the other half is pinpointing the sins of others, your whole life is full of fear and condemnation.

June 24

Those who are led by the Spirit of God are the children of God. The Spirit you received does not make you slaves, so that you live in fear again; rather ... The Spirit himself testifies with our spirit that we are God's children. (Romans 8:14–16)

June 25

Salvation is simple: you're either in or out. There's no teetering on the edge. There's no borderline. And there's no question: if you're covered by the blood of Jesus then you rest safely in His grace.

❧

June 26

The grace of God is a spring that flows from inside His heart—and it never runs dry.

June 27

Grace is the currency that pays for sin. The sacrificed body of Jesus fills your spiritual account with a permanent supply of grace. Therefore, you will never receive a bill demanding payment for your sins, because an eternal deposit has already been made on your behalf.

June 28

God's grace is more powerful than any doubts or discouragements. Hold onto grace in perseverance because it always overcomes doubt and restores you to a healthy state of faith.

June 29

And we know that in all things God works for the good of those who love him, who have been called according to his purpose. For those God foreknew he also predestined to be conformed to the image of his Son ... And those he predestined, he also called; those he called, he also justified; those he justified, he also glorified. What, then, shall we say in response to these things? If God is for us, who can be against us? (Romans 8:28–31)

June 30

Prepare for the worst, pray for the best, and expect God in the end.

July 1

In general, it seems that God doesn't give us everything we want and then ask us to consider obeying Him. Typically, upon consistent obedience from the heart, we seem to "run into" a blessing that God has for us. Often times, these blessings exist only in the *center* of His will. When we obey the Spirit, one moment at a time, we will be in that center.

***

July 2

Authentic obedience is not the act of it, but the heart behind it.

July 3

I do not care if I am judged by you ... I do not even judge myself ... The Lord is the One who judges me. So do not judge before the right time; wait until the Lord comes. He will bring to light things that are now hidden in darkness, and will make known the secret purposes of people's hearts. (1 Corinthians 4:3–5)

July 4

If you love and pursue the godly things, you will receive all the things you need on this earth. On the contrary, if you love and pursue the earthly, it will not give you the godly in return.

July 5

Do not love the world or the things in the world. If you love the world, the love of the Father is not in you. These are the ways of the world: wanting to please our sinful selves, wanting the sinful things we see, and being too proud of what we have. None of these come from the Father, but all of them come from the world. The world and everything in it are passing away, but the person who does what God wants lives forever. (1 John 2:15–17 NCV)

July 6

Some people rationalize their personal obsessions as God's will for them; or they believe the things they obsess over are the passions that God has put in their heart. But obsessions are not passions. Obsessions come and go, often born from earthly desires. But a God-given passion lasts forever and eventually brings long-term purpose.

July 7

All who make themselves clean from evil will be used for special purposes. They will be made holy, useful to the Master, ready to do any good work. (2 Timothy 2:21 NCV)

July 8

If you honestly pursue the Lord today, then there's nothing to fear about tomorrow.

July 9

Now is the only present tense there will ever be. Don't waste it by worrying about the future or dwelling on the past. Learn from your past and plan for your future, but live for today.

⌘

July 10

> Trust in the Lord and do good ... Take delight in the Lord, and he will give you the desires of your heart. Commit your way to the Lord; trust in him and he will do this: He will make your righteous reward shine like the dawn, your vindication like the noonday sun. Be still before the Lord and wait patiently for him; do not fret. (Psalm 37:3–7)

July 11

Most of the time, when we think it's time to act, even before things are made clear, all we need to do is wait a little longer. In fact, a good rule to live by is this: when you think you can't wait another minute, hold on for just one more.

July 12

Do not be afraid. Stand firm and you will see the deliverance the Lord will bring you ... The Lord will fight for you; you need only to be still. (Exodus 14:13–14)

July 13

Practice faithfulness and wisdom in the smaller things so you can be ready for the bigger things. Everything today is preparing you for tomorrow. Develop yourself as if your future depends on it, because it does! Your opportunities are coming, so get ready.

July 14

Restrain your voice from weeping and your eyes from tears, for your work will be rewarded ... There is hope for your future. (Jeremiah 31:16–17)

July 15

Heartbreak is an opportunity to find out who God really is—not in the breaking of your heart, but in the healing of it. During the healing process, you will find new strength and a new direction.

⚬⌾⊰§⊱⌾⚬

July 16

> This is what the Lord says ... "Forget the former things; do not dwell on the past. See, I am doing a new thing! Now it springs up; do you not perceive it? I am making a way." (Isaiah 43:16–19)

July 17

Lord God, remember me. God, please give me strength one more time. (Judges 16:28 NCV)

July 18

There's a stark contrast between following your heart and listening to your emotions. You cannot follow your heart until you've pinpointed the difference between human desire and the deep inner path that God has placed inside of you. Seek the Lord and He will reveal your path to you in His timing. But in the meantime, do not follow your emotions or make decisions based on them. Allow God the time to cut through the fog of your feelings to show you the truth.

July 19

Your road led through the sea, your pathway through the mighty waters—a pathway no one knew was there. (Psalm 77:19 NLT)

July 20

As responsible, God-fearing adults, we have tough decisions to make. And sometimes it's difficult to pull the trigger and do the right thing when we care too much about what other people think. But when we do what God wants—no matter what anyone else thinks—it is best for *everyone* in the long run.

Do you think I am trying to make people accept me? No, God is the One I am trying to please. Am I trying to please people? If I still wanted to please people, I would not be a servant of Christ. (Galatians 1:10 NCV)

Servants of Christ follow Jesus and hope to get others to follow Him. But servants of self are more interested in getting people to follow them.

July 23

Sometimes we confuse the ones with the strongest personalities or most interesting arguments as the ones who are strongest in the faith and worthy of following. Although there's nothing wrong with a strong personality, charismatic presence, or clever Biblical inspiration (if done responsibly and without motive), those are not reasons to follow a human being (1 Corinthians 3:1–11). We are to follow Jesus only. Of course He places "leaders" in our midst. But legitimate Christian leaders don't actually lead; *they follow* the lead of Jesus. They follow Him in everyday life and character, and they make decisions based on obedience to Him through God's Word and the Holy Spirit. The goal for *every* Christian, whether in a position of leadership or not, should be to live for Jesus, inside and out, to the best of their ability in whatever capacity they serve.

⁂

July 24

You don't need to be as innocent as Mary to be pure enough. You don't need to be as merciful as the Good Samaritan to love enough. You don't need to be as prayerful as John to be spiritual enough. We try so hard to be pure enough, spiritual enough, prayerful enough, loving enough, kind enough. Obviously those are good goals; but it's not healthy to aim for those goals without being firmly entrenched in this truth: Jesus makes you more than enough.

July 25

Spiritual freedom will only come once you're secure enough in Jesus to trust Him to be your only source of salvation and righteousness. In other words, you must let go of all spiritual control, disconnect yourself from factoring into your faith, and trust the blood of Jesus to be your single hope for heaven and personal holiness. You have to take yourself completely out of the equation in order to live freely by faith in Jesus Christ.

July 26

Fear and faith are polar opposites. The more faith you have, the less fear you have.

July 27

Stress is a response to life. *Your* stress level is your response to your life. If you are too stressed, then you should change how you respond to life, or you should respond by making some changes.

July 28

> The righteous cry out, and the Lord hears them; he delivers them from all their troubles. The Lord is close to the brokenhearted and saves those who are crushed in spirit. The righteous person may have many troubles, but the Lord delivers him from them all. (Psalm 34:17–19)

July 29

God not only loves you, He likes you. Let me repeat that: God likes you. He delights in you. He takes pleasure in you. God smiles when He thinks of you. This means He never stops smiling, because He's always thinking of you. Indeed, the day you were born, God beamed with joy. He didn't need to create you, but He certainly chose to.

⁓⧉⁓

July 30

In adult life, the simplicity of childhood gets left far behind. That's why Jesus says we are to *change* and go back to being like a child (Matthew 18:3–4). Not *childish*, but *childlike*. We are to live with childlike faith, dependence, and humility. Like children, we are to believe everything that God says. We are to rely on Him for provision and essentials. We should always feel safe and know that God has us in the palm of His hands. And, as if we see through the eyes of children, we should gaze upon our Father as our hero.

July 31

As God's child, by definition, you are not the breadwinner of the arrangement. You are not responsible for earning an eternal living. Rather, you are the child that God feeds and protects. You are the one He delights in. You are the one He died for.

August 1

(Gentiles) were made right with God because of their faith. The people of Israel tried to follow a law to make themselves right with God. But they did not succeed, because they tried to make themselves right by the things they did, instead of trusting in God to make them right. (Romans 9:30–32 NCV)

August 2

Grace is a handout from God. Will you take it or say *no thanks?*

⚜

August 3

After two thousand years of meddling with the gospel of grace, humans have managed to complicate it. But make no mistake; this is the simple good news:

You are saved by grace through faith in Jesus Christ.

Although it seems logical to include impeccable performance and advanced theology as part of the gospel, they aren't.

August 4

If we aren't teaching grace, then we aren't teaching Christianity. Without grace, the cross of Christ is meaningless and the love of God is a distant theology.

August 5

Prophecy and speaking in unknown languages and special knowledge will become useless. But love will last forever! Now our knowledge is partial and incomplete, and ... we see things imperfectly ... (But) three things will last forever—faith, hope, and love—and the greatest of these is love. (So) *let love be your highest goal.* (1 Corinthians 13:8–14:1 NLT)

God's love forgives you and doesn't track your mistakes. As you mature in His love, you will learn how to forgive others in that same way. Indeed, the signature of maturation in God's love is to stop keeping inventory of the sins and errors of everyone else.

> Above all, love each other deeply, because love covers over a multitude of sins. (1 Peter 4:8)

> You were cleansed from your sins when you obeyed the truth, so now you must show sincere love to each other as brothers and sisters. Love each other deeply with all your heart. (1 Peter 1:22 NLT)

August 8

Just like a machine needs every part to function properly and operate in unison to run at its highest capacity, the church needs to work together in love, as a unit, to be stronger and more productive for the Lord (Ecclesiastes 4:9–12; Ephesians 4:11–16).

August 9

To become the functional body of Christ on earth would require each of us to love our neighbors; to overlook offenses without judgment; to forgive; to be merciful; to not expect perfection; and to accept others—even though they don't deserve it—as Christ has accepted us. To put it simply: To be the body of Christ requires Christ-like becoming of us.

August 10

Let's worry less about what we preach and concentrate more on practicing it.

⚜

August 11

> I am not writing you a new command but one we
> have had from the beginning. I ask that we love one
> another. And this is love: that we walk in obedience
> to his commands. As you have heard from the
> beginning, his command is that you walk in love. (2
> John verses 5–6)

August 12

Love-based obedience is consumed with Jesus and gladly follows Him in a spirit of gratitude. On the contrary, performance-based obedience gets locked in on the act of obedience itself.

⁓⊱✦⊰⁓

August 13

Humans will always fail and slump. That means you and I will drop the ball, even when we try not to. But these slumps do not condemn us; they only discourage us. And nagging discouragements are temporary setbacks, not death sentences. So we must resist the feelings of condemnation that sometimes accompany our slumps, because such feelings are not based on truth (Romans 8:1). The truth is Jesus conquered our sins forever! The cross does not lose its power when we fail. Nothing can change what Jesus did for us, and His blood is more powerful than any sin or slump will ever be.

Salvation occurs in a moment, but growth never ends. Failure is necessary for growth, so be prepared for it. You will fail at some point. But growing pains and failures do not endanger your salvation, so don't let your mistakes keep you down.

Though I have fallen, I will rise. (Micah 7:8)

Though the righteous fall (numerous) times, they rise again. (Proverbs 24:16)

August 15

Don't let yourself imagine that God keeps a running tab on how many times He has to forgive you. He's not keeping track. It may be hard to fathom that the blood of Jesus covers you with a constant amount of grace—whether you have one sin or a million—but it's vital that you do.

August 16

We all want to be holy, but we can't let personal holiness get entangled with why we're forgiven. Our sins aren't pardoned because we deserve it, but because Jesus does.

～⊹⊱✦⊰⊹～

August 17

Grace is not selective as we often imagine it to be. God doesn't punch a calculator and tally up our sins to see who deserves heaven the most. Nor does He pick and choose between sets of believers, weighing the accuracy of one group's theological studies with the fervency of another group's prayers. Such detailed scrutiny does not exist. God either sees Jesus in someone or He doesn't. There is no right versus wrong, good versus bad checklist. Life is a simple pass/fail course, and there is only one question on the final exam:

"Do you have Jesus?"

Heaven is not for the most deserving. It's for those in whom the Holy Spirit dwells.

Christian obedience is a byproduct of the Spirit-filled and loving heart, not a standard by which we are measured.

August 20

Should politicians serve the political platform of their party or the people who elected them? Similarly, should Christians serve their precise doctrines or the Christ who saves them?

⚜

August 21

Almost without exception, everyone in the world is desperate for acceptance. They're desperate for approval. Little do they know they're actually desperate for Jesus. They long for His love, but they just don't know it. If they could only see that He has everything they need. If they could only see that *we* have everything they need. If they could only see God's grace at work in us, leaving no doubts about the truth of His love and no doubts that we have what they're desperate for.

> The grace of the Lord Jesus be with God's people. Amen. (Revelation 22:21)

In order to reach all types of people we have to accept all types of people. Our goal is not to win the lost so we can strap them down in our laboratories and transform them into us. We can't all be alike, nor are we designed to be. We are individual brainstorms by God, uniquely constructed beings. In order to know God's unconditional love, every one of us must be free to be ourselves.

August 23

The advanced stage of love is to keep no record of wrongs. It is to overlook the things that make people different than you. It is to love unconditionally.

August 24

To *love* does not mean *to approve*. Love is able to separate the sin from the sinner. The Spirit's love teaches us to overlook the faults of others, not with negligence or ignorance, but mercy. We learn how to truly forgive everyone—not because we approve of them, but because we don't judge them. In fact, such forgiveness without judgment is required of us if we hope to be forgiven without judgment ourselves (Matthew 6:15; 7:1).

August 25

God loved the world so much that he gave his one and only Son so that whoever believes in him may not be lost, but have eternal life. God did not send his Son into the world to judge the world guilty, but to save the world through him. (John 3:16–17 NCV)

August 26

When you analyze Jesus to pieces, all that you find is love. What would we find in you?

❧

August 27

> This is what the Lord says: "Don't let the wise boast in their wisdom, or the powerful boast in their power, or the rich boast in their riches. But those who wish to boast should boast in this alone: that they truly know me and understand that I am the Lord who demonstrates unfailing love and who brings justice and righteousness to the earth, and that I delight in these things." (Jeremiah 9:23–24 NLT)

August 28

Your priorities must be defined by things of eternal value—things like spiritual growth and love—not earthly gain, which is measured by treasure or social popularity. Of course you have to pay your bills and it's important to have a good reputation, but don't make your life decisions based on *earthly gain* or any other patterns of the world. You will lose the game of life if you pour yourself into anything but your faith and family.

⸎

August 29

To grow your faith and strengthen your family on a daily basis has nothing to do with bustling activity. To taxi your kids from place to place does very little for your relationships and development. Any personal growth—whether with God or family—occurs with significant quantities of quality time, which doesn't exist in a time-crunched environment. Developing and strengthening your faith and family are not timeslots on your appointment calendar to squeeze into your busy life—they are the only things on your calendar that really matter. But such priority systems never materialize in those who are swallowed up by the hectic pace of this world or governed by what it says is important.

Brothers and sisters, look at what you were when God called you. Not many of you were wise in the way the world judges wisdom. Not many of you had great influence. Not many of you came from important families. But God chose the foolish things of the world to shame the wise, and he chose the weak things of the world to shame the strong. He chose what the world thinks is unimportant and what the world looks down on and thinks is nothing in order to destroy what the world thinks is important. (1 Corinthians 1:26–28 NCV)

August 31

To be stable in the eyes of the world is to be unstable in soul and spirit.

September 1

Nothing in all the world can be hidden from God. Everything is clear and lies open before him, and to him we must explain the way we have lived. (Hebrews 4:13 NCV)

September 2

A greedy person is an idolater, worshiping the things of this world. Don't be fooled by those who try to excuse these sins. (Ephesians 5:5–6 NLT)

September 3

Being grateful is the secret to fulfillment. Those who are grateful don't covet. In other words, they want what they already have.

❧

September 4

> Keep your lives free from the love of money and be content with what you have. (Hebrews 13:5)

September 5

I have learned to be content whatever the circumstances ... God will meet all your needs according to the riches of his glory in Christ Jesus. (Philippians 4:11, 19)

∼∞✠∞∼

September 6

Gratitude sees the bright side of things, which fundamentally opens your eyes to possibility and hope, all while being content in heart for where God has you right now.

September 7

I did not come preaching God's secret with fancy words or a show of human wisdom. I decided that while I was with you I would forget about everything except Jesus Christ and his death on the cross. So when I came to you, I was weak and fearful and trembling. My teaching and preaching were not with words of human wisdom that persuade people but with proof of the power that the Spirit gives. This was so that your faith would be in God's power and not in human wisdom. (1 Corinthians 2:1–5 NCV)

September 8

Great religious knowledge (as important as it may be) can be a path to pride; so be on guard against this kind of pride and the spiritual stagnation of the heart that often accompanies it. Though it isn't good to be uninformed, a hardened heart is disastrous.

September 9

Doctrines and interpretations make for interesting philosophical and theological discussions, but they are practically irrelevant in the pursuit of Christ.

September 10

> I want you to remember the Good News I brought to you. You received this Good News and continue strong in it. And you are being saved by it if you continue believing what I told you. If you do not, then you believed for nothing. I passed on to you what I received, of which this was most important: that Christ died for our sins. (1 Corinthians 15:1–3 NCV)

September 11

On earth, it is the design of God that we work for what we get (2 Thessalonians 3:10–12; 1 Thessalonians 4:11–12). But eternally speaking, Jesus did the work for what we get.

～✥～

September 12

We must learn to put our entire faith in Jesus and leave self out of the equation. We must grow beyond the point of giving credence to us and the things we do. Jesus is the one who gets all the credit for getting things right. Perhaps that's the problem for some of us. Perhaps, as humans, we want some of the credit. But the Bible is very clear: By supreme design, grace eliminates all bragging rights from us and alleviates the pressure to get things right (Ephesians 2:8–9). Part of grace's deal was to crucify the notion of creditworthiness and strip away all human acclaim so we would stop reaching for religious achievement and start honoring Jesus for who He is and cherishing Him for what He's done.

September 13

We cannot earn any more credit than what our faith in Christ already grants us. We cannot give God reasons to love us more than He already does. We cannot make ourselves more acceptable than what Jesus already has. So unless you quit trying to earn whatever it is you're trying to earn, and unless you quit trying to hold up the end of a bargain that Jesus already did, you won't comprehend the spiritual freedom that you've been promised. "The truth that sets you free" is not available unless you throw yourself out of the game of religion and into the arms of Jesus.

September 14

You cannot contain the brightness of life and newness of heart that occurs in those who escape the grasp of religious rules. True life in the Spirit cannot occur until you realize that all those external rules of religion—foods, rituals, dress codes, rights and wrongs, dos and don'ts—hold you back, bog you down, *and put too much focus on you.* Such rules are props that you don't need anymore. They're like crutches for one who can walk without them—they serve no purpose and slow you down. Fully grown spiritual freedom rids itself of all such props and crutches, because it's been released from the captivity of performance-centered religion and doesn't want it back. Freedom wants no part of the fruitless efforts to please God with religious regulations, but rather lives confidently and contently in Christ and puts *absolute* faith in Him.

September 15

> Who has held you back from following the truth? It
> certainly isn't God, for he is the one who called you
> to freedom. (Galatians 5:7–8 NLT)

ᘓᘓᘓᘓᘓᘓ

September 16

There are some brothers and sisters in Christ who redefine freedom
in order to believe they live in it. Often times, a good indicator of
false freedom is when religious rules are a source of division within
the kingdom, such that identities are more tied to distinctive beliefs
than our Savior. A willingness to quarrel and divide over fine-print
doctrines screams a lack of freedom and suggests one's faith to be in
something other than Christ; or, at the very least, it implies one to be
quite sidetracked from the gospel of God's liberating grace and the
heart of His unconditional love.

You have been called to live in freedom, my brothers and sisters. But don't use your freedom to satisfy your sinful nature. Instead, use your freedom to serve one another in love. For the whole law can be summed up in this one command: "Love your neighbor as yourself." (Galatians 5:13–14 NLT)

September 18

There is no *effort* to give God glory and affection once freedom enters the picture. Love for God and others is an *uncontrollable response* at the point of realized freedom.

September 19

Accept the one whose faith is weak, without quarreling over disputable matters. One person's faith allows them to eat anything, but another, whose faith is weak, eats only vegetables (a restricted diet, for religious reasons). The one who eats everything must not treat with contempt the one who does not, and the one who does not eat everything must not judge the one who does, for God has accepted them. (Romans 14:1–3)

September 20

Other Christians aren't the lost, no matter what you have been taught to believe. Energy is more wisely spent trying to convert unbelievers, rather than attempting to convince other Christians to see things your way.

September 21

Having an opinion is one thing; being opinionated is another.

⚬⟳⟊⟡⟲⚬

September 22

I'm not a medical expert, but because of the serious nature of operating on a heart, I assume these surgeries are not done in haste. With that in mind, would it not be reasonable to be patient with God—your heart Surgeon—if your heart seems painfully slow to heal or isn't soft enough or pure enough?

September 23

As God's "patient" there is nothing more important than being patient.

❧

September 24

Tireless effort to be the best Christian won't get you where you want to go or make you who you want to be. However, faith in the Holy Spirit to make you more like Jesus will produce positive changes in your life; especially if your focus isn't on your progress, but on your Savior.

Perhaps you can relate to these two imaginary boxes of mine.

> Box One is labeled "Marcus Bradley." It is filled with my utter existence.

> Box Two is labeled "What Marcus Bradley always felt he must do in order to be accepted." This box contains my interpretation of who I should be or want to be. This fake person is largely based on image and/or my ability to be nearly perfect.

Box One is filled to the brim with God's love. In other words, God loves me because I am. Conversely, Box Two is empty. There is no substance to it. You must realize that God loves your *person*, but He can care less about your *persona*.

I lived many years worried that I wasn't good enough or wasn't doing everything right. I didn't feel securely accepted by God. I didn't trust in His love. I guess I was too scared to believe it was unconditional. But it is. The real me is truly loved without stipulation. And so is the real you.

September 27

Until you accept yourself fully, you won't be able to receive all the love that God has reserved for you. You must know and believe that you don't need to be sinless to be lovable. You don't need to be blemish-free, in any way, to be lovable. You only need to be *you* to be lovable.

❦

September 28

God loves you so much that He gives you the credit for the holiness that Christ achieved (see Romans 4:23–25).

September 29

Each of us is "graded" equally on what I call *the mercy curve*. We all get straight A's. We are deemed perfect because of God's immeasurable mercy.

September 30

> But because of his great love for us, God, who is rich in mercy, made us alive in Christ even when we were dead in transgressions—it is by grace you have been saved. (Ephesians 2:4–5)

October 1

As new Christians begin to follow Jesus, it's imperative they understand God's grace; because when they mess up, they need to be repentant, not fearful.

October 2

In the very center of God's heart, you will find inconceivable amounts of mercy that allow Him to overlook all of your faults with genuine love and purity.

October 3

May the Lord make your love increase and overflow for each other and for everyone else, just as ours does for you. May he strengthen your hearts so that you will be blameless and holy in the presence of our God and Father when our Lord Jesus comes. (1 Thessalonians 3:12–13)

∽⊙⧫⊙∾

October 4

Life can be disappointing, at times. Not to sound negative, but graveyards are full of unfulfilled hopes, dreams, and expectations. Life goes unfinished. Bucket lists stay full. There is always more to do. It's extremely rare for a person to accomplish everything they want in this life, but I think that's how it's supposed to be. This life is a preparation for the next. We won't be fully satisfied until heaven. But there is a big difference between satisfaction and contentment. By the strength of Christ Jesus, we can be—and should be—entirely content without being perfectly satisfied on earth.

October 5

Most of us look forward to the journey of life—particularly in anticipation of certain milestones and breakthroughs—but let us not forget the part of life we call "today"; because today is, by far, the most important leg of the voyage.

❧

October 6

It's better to be grateful that you have something to anticipate, than to anticipate that you'll one day have reason to be grateful.

October 7

Sometimes moving forward takes time. As much as we don't like to hear it, time gives God the opportunity to teach us the things we need to know before we can move onto the next stage of life. Periods of waiting can be extremely difficult to endure. Waiting too long (or what *feels* too long) creates a sense of desperation and, often times, loneliness. Sometimes it takes everything you can muster to wait on God and His timing without losing your cool, or even your faith.

When God is silent, it's hard to believe that He's still there. But He is. During times of what seems like nothingness, it's very natural for doubts to creep in (or storm in). Every bit of you wants God to show up and do something...*anything*. But if the silence persists, do your best to rest in His Word. Know that God is working hard behind the scenes on your behalf. He has an unwavering plan for you. And it's going to happen.

❧❦❧

October 8

> Can a mother forget the baby at her breast and have no compassion on the child she has borne? Though she may forget, I will not forget you! See, I have engraved you on the palms of my hands. (Isaiah 49:15–16)

To live by faith is not to force your way and believe that everything will turn out fine. It's to be patient with God as you wait for things to develop. Faith resists the temptation to stop waiting and go in *some* direction, because faith knows the wisdom of the *right* direction. To live by faith is to persevere and trust that God knows what He's doing, even if nothing is happening or making sense. And faith, in spite of not *seeing* anything happen in your favor, prepares for the day when God decides to move. So be ready in faith for your day to come. Make use of your time as you wait. Be disciplined in your preparations. Endure to the end. Don't give up and don't stop preparing. God is going to move. Will you be ready to go with Him?

⸎

October 10

Trust in the Lord with all your heart and lean not on your own understanding; in all your ways submit to him, and he will make your paths straight. (Proverbs 3:5–6)

October 11

It cannot be assumed that resistance is an obstacle to overcome. Sometimes it's a warning. It could be a word of caution that is advising you to slow down or to stop altogether and digest things. Whatever the resistance, you should always wait until you know its purpose before proceeding.

∞⊷⊶∞

October 12

You can't listen to God unless you are completely honest with yourself in every area of life. Without pure honesty at the core of your being, you can simply claim (and even believe) that God has told you to do whatever it is you want to do.

October 13

It's your obligation to try your best to be a great Christian and follow God, but that's not really possible if your motor is being fueled by human endeavor.

Cﾑﾑﾑﾑﾑﾑﾑﾑﾑﾑﾑﾑﾑ

October 14

The world believes all your time and focus should be on yourself, your career, and your ability to provide the nicest things for your family, all while building a retirement cache large enough to live luxuriously until you are 120 years old; and they say to do otherwise is foolishness. Well, I'm okay with being called a fool by the world's standards. And to be honest, I've spent some time living the worldly kind of life built around money. But eventually—and thankfully—I found the world of money to be profoundly empty.

October 15

Command those who are rich with things of this world not to be proud. Tell them to hope in God, not in their uncertain riches. God richly gives us everything to enjoy. Tell the rich people to do good, to be rich in doing good deeds, to be generous and ready to share. By doing that, they will be saving a treasure for themselves as a strong foundation for the future. Then they will be able to have the life that is true life. (1 Timothy 6:17–19 NCV)

October 16

Ask a rich unbeliever on his deathbed if he's satisfied. How can he be? He's got nothing to look forward to and he's about to lose all he ever had.

In his distress he sought the favor of the Lord his God and humbled himself greatly ... (Therefore) when he prayed to him, the Lord was moved by his entreaty and listened to his plea. (2 Chronicles 33:12–13)

⁓⦂⦂⦂⦂⁓

The self-worth of a Christian obviously doesn't come from earthly success, the fruits of which ultimately burn. But nor does a Christian's value come from spiritual success, which is loosely defined by growing in love, truth, holiness, and fruitfulness. As essential as those things are, your self-worth is not tied to them. Your self-worth is embedded solely in the crown of thorns, the pierced side, and the holes in the wrists and feet of your Savior. Your value is found at the foot of the cross—Jesus died for you; God forgives you; He loves you forever.

October 19

Do you want success? Do you want significance? Listen to these words:

> Jesus called out your name as He emerged from the tomb. No other name was shouted before yours. You are the first thing on His mind every day, all the time—always have been and always will be. Nothing matters more than you. You are worth saving. You are worth loving. You are worth *dying for*. You are important enough to be exchanged for the life—and death—of Jesus. *God's high opinion of you is equally unfathomable as it is undeniable.*

❧

October 20

You cannot earn significance. You merely accept it.

October 21

Time wasted meditating on trivial matters—which includes over-thinking spiritual things—is time you will never get back.

❦

October 22

I am loved regardless of how much I figure out.

October 23

Jesus came to release us from stringent demands, procedures, and regulations. He can't bear to see us in those chains. He can't bear to see us struggling in deep thought over the proper way to do this and the correct way to do that. Life in the Spirit is not about those things. Christianity is not about those things. It's about Jesus Christ and His undying love for you.

October 24

There's nothing wrong with religious rules or deep spiritual thinking until they take your focus away from the cross, which they inevitably do.

October 25

> A person may think their own ways are right, but the
> Lord weighs the heart. (Proverbs 21:2)

October 26

To pour your heart and soul into the best religious practices is to risk them becoming too important.

October 27

Make no mistake about it. Jesus is in direct competition with your religious rules in this regard: He wants your faith and attention to be on Him, not them. Christians have a hard time resisting the nature to elevate ourselves—even if subconsciously—based on our specific religious beliefs. This self-elevation, which is sneaky and usually arises out of good intentions to do things the right way, is plainly manifested by the hundreds of different church brands that all believe in Jesus but are divided because the details of our doctrines are a little different. Gross negligence aside, there is no reason to divide over doctrine. A perfect doctrine does not exist, nor does a perfect church. Only a perfect Savior.

October 28

If you succeed at following all the rules and rites you can find, you'll still be imperfect. But through Christ, you are absolutely perfect and completely saved (Hebrews 7:25).

October 29

> You, Lord, give true peace to those who depend on
> you, because they trust you. (Isaiah 26:3 NCV)

⸎

October 30

You have nothing to fear because Jesus is your hope (Hebrews 6:19–
20). God's grace is sufficient for you through the blood of Christ (2
Corinthians 12:9). There's no need to continually qualify for salvation:

> We have been made holy through the sacrifice of the
> body of Jesus Christ once for all. (Hebrews 10:10)

October 31

Jesus is not standing on the sidelines waiting for you to sin before He enters the game.

⁘

November 1

> Because He Himself suffered when He was tempted,
> He is able to help those who are being tempted.
> (Hebrews 2:18)

November 2

Obedience to Christ improves when it's a reaction to His loving Spirit rather than a controlled effort of the flesh.

❦

November 3

Although we put no hope in our actions, we are to do everything out of worship. As meager as they are, our actions and procedures are a form of devotion. Even though they are ultimately meaningless, our actions are all that we have to offer to say, "thank You, Lord, for saving me."

God has always lived with us. From the Garden of Eden, to the burning bush, to the Ark of the Covenant, to the temple, God has always been near. But apparently, it wasn't near enough for His liking, because He chose to become flesh and live a human life alongside of us. Upon completion of His life on earth, when Jesus ascended to heaven, God took it a step further: He sent His Holy Spirit to dwell *inside of us* (Acts 2:33), such that *we are God's dwelling place* (Ephesians 2:22). We are His house (1 Peter 2:5). We are the temple (1 Corinthians 3:16; 6:19). Jesus is the cornerstone of God's temple, the apostles and prophets are the foundation, and we are the building (Ephesians 2:20–22).

The purpose of God sending His Holy Spirit to dwell inside of you is nothing new. God's desire has not changed since the beginning: He wants to be close to you. And now He's inside of you. You are God's *home*. So make Him feel welcome by the way that you live.

⟳⟳⟳⟳

God called us to be holy and does not want us to live in sin. (1 Thessalonians 4:7 NCV)

There's nothing wrong with good old-fashioned obedience by willpower. It's worth something to do the right thing because you know that you should. But how long will that last? I guess some people can go on forever like that. But the way I see it, the most effective method of obedience is a Spirit-led, heartfelt obedience from a liberated soul who loves to please the Lord.

November 7

Obedience is not a prerequisite for salvation, but a result of it.

November 8

You can't believe everything that you hear; particularly in the tones they are delivered.

⚜

November 9

One form of evangelism is from the pulpit, but I think most preachers and evangelists would agree—real evangelism occurs in our everyday lives and relationships.

In John chapter thirteen, Jesus declared that loving each other will prove to the world that we are God's people. He didn't say gimmicks, rhetoric, apologetics, theology, intelligent sermons, or anything else will prove us as His own. He said love will.

> Love one another. As I have loved you, so you must love one another. By this everyone will know you are my disciples, if you love one another. (John 13:34–35)

November 11

Individuals who experience God's grace firsthand by accepting His forgiveness—first inwardly for self, then extending it to others—is what builds up the body of Christ as the powerful unit we're designed to be.

November 12

Knowledge puffs up while love builds up.
(1 Corinthians 8:1)

When our love is real, people will want what we have. When we love one another from the inside, then changes will happen on the outside—changes like reflecting Christ and winning lost souls for Him.

***

November 13

Love prospers when a fault is forgiven, but dwelling on it separates close friends. (Proverbs 17:9 NLT)

Eternal life is not about our favorite traditions, spiritual gifts, or even becoming a holier person; and it certainly isn't about fearing hell, decoding prophecies, or spotlighting the end times. It's about the blood of Jesus Christ and the love that was displayed on Calvary.

November 15

Good and upright is the Lord; therefore He instructs sinners in His ways. He guides the humble in what is right and teaches them His way. All the ways of the Lord are loving and faithful. (Psalm 25:8–10)

Trying to be confident leads to arrogance. Attempting to be humble gives birth to pride. Only when you rest in the grace of Christ are you confident and humble at the same time.

To trust in the grace of Christ is to acknowledge that *you* don't play a role in salvation, and that is the basis of a Christian's humility. Furthermore, to be certain that Jesus is perfect enough to save you is to trust Him with your life, and that is the source of a Christian's confidence. In Jesus you will find both humility and confidence. On the contrary, in strict religion you will find pride and fear.

November 17

But blessed are those who trust in the Lord and have made the Lord their hope and confidence. They are like trees planted along a riverbank, with roots that reach deep into the water. Such trees are not bothered by the heat or worried by long months of drought. Their leaves stay green, and they never stop producing fruit. (Jeremiah 17:7–8 NLT)

November 18

Life is how we deal with things, not what we have to deal with.

⁓

November 19

God is our refuge and strength, an ever-present help in trouble. Therefore we will not fear. (Psalm 46:1–2)

If faith heals, then fear sickens.

⚜

I will glory in the Lord; let the afflicted hear and rejoice. Glorify the Lord with me; let us exalt his name together. I sought the Lord, and he answered me; he delivered me from all my fears. (Psalm 34:2–4)

November 22

When we doubt, we stand at a crossroad. We can back off and listen to fear, or we can believe that anything is possible with God. There will be times of anxiety and long stretches of waiting, but the key is to never give up. Patience and perseverance always overcome doubt in the end.

❧

November 23

This is what the Lord God, the Holy One of Israel, says: "If you come back to me and trust me, you will be saved. If you will be calm and trust me, you will be strong." (Isaiah 30:15 NCV)

November 24

The more you think about your problems, the longer they stick around.

⸎⸎⸎⸎

November 25

When times are tough, things always seem to get better as soon as I take the focus off of me and put it onto others.

November 26

Giving thanks delivers you from life's ruts.

⁂

November 27

Do everything without complaining or arguing. (Philippians 2:14 NCV)

Do everything in love. (1 Corinthians 16:14 NCV)

November 28

In my life, I have learned that the term "quality of life" has nothing to do with the things that money can buy.

❧

November 29

It takes more faith to be patient than to suppose quick action in your favor.

The faith to start something is noble, but the perseverance to see it through to completion is much more gratifying.

> The end of a matter is better than its beginning, and patience is better than pride. (Ecclesiastes 7:8)

December 1

The most faithful and spiritual among us are not those who try to figure out all the signs and answers. They do not suffer from *paralysis by analysis*, nor do they dwell on what God may or may not do. They are not concerned with the things that most of us fret over, because they have learned to let everything go and leave it all up to God.

December 2

> The Lord is a refuge for the oppressed, a stronghold in times of trouble. Those who know your name trust in you, for you, Lord, have never forsaken those who seek you. (Psalm 9:9–10)

December 3

Good intentions and religious quests can take you down a million paths, but seeking Jesus Christ will always steer you to the forgiving love of God and re-center you on the gospel of your hope.

December 4

Therefore, my dear brothers and sisters, stand firm. Let nothing move you. Always give yourselves fully to the work of the Lord, because you know that your labor in the Lord is not in vain. (1 Corinthians 15:58)

December 5

Peter experienced exponential growth in his life of service. He always tried to do the right thing, but he didn't always do things with the right heart. Eventually, as he grew in the grace of the Lord, His heart came all the way around to be in sync with God. To be precise, Peter evolved from judging others in his ministry (evidence of knowing right from wrong in his head) to tolerating them (evidence of beginning to mature in his heart) to loving them (evidence of a life immersed in the Spirit). He even came so far as to accept the Gentile Christians (Acts 10:28), who were unlike him in every way. By observing the ministry of Peter, we can see that once we are able to tolerate, love, and accept the Christ-followers who are different than us, we, too, will be graduating beyond human nature and into the Spirit's love.

December 6

A person's wisdom yields patience; it is to one's glory
to overlook an offense. (Proverbs 19:11)

⚬⚬⚬⚬⚬⚬

December 7

Differences of opinion don't demand division.

Peter and Paul disagreed about some things, but they wholeheartedly agreed that Jesus was the Messiah. Therefore, they remained yoked in the faith, in spite of their differences. So it's okay that we don't agree on everything—details of Christian theology, church service styles, etc. We're still in this thing together serving the One Savior, Jesus Christ.

December 9

You have been called by God to be his own holy people. He made you holy by means of Christ Jesus, just as he did for all people everywhere who call on the name of our Lord Jesus Christ, their Lord and ours. (1 Corinthians 1:2 NLT)

December 10

The followers of Christ are not to quarrel, because it's impossible to represent Him if we bicker and take sides.

⁕

December 11

> Don't have anything to do with foolish and stupid arguments, because you know they produce quarrels. And the Lord's servant must not be quarrelsome. (2 Timothy 2:23–24)

December 12

Find a church that makes you feel comfortable enough to worship the Lord in peace. And if you can't find any place good enough for you, then maybe you should re-evaluate yourself or your expectations a bit.

December 13

You are to have sober judgment of yourself (Romans 12:3)—not too high, not too low. Not blinded by self, imagining you're better than others; yet not slumping in pity, thinking others are better than you.

December 14

The church of academia and the church of raw emotion—both have a place, but we really need equilibrium between the two.

❧

December 15

Balance the heart and head: if you're all heart, you can't follow a straight path; but all head, often times, leads to rigidity.

December 16

Faith cannot be tied to self, in any way. Jesus Christ must be your wholehearted Savior, the totality of your faith.

⌒⌒⊗⊹⊹⊗⌒⌒

December 17

> Brothers, understand what we are telling you: You can have forgiveness of your sins through Jesus. The Law of Moses could not free you from your sins. But through Jesus everyone who believes is free from all sins. (Acts 13:38–39 NCV)

December 18

I call the grace of God through Jesus Christ, *grace for no reason.* It takes childlike faith to believe in such a thing.

❧

December 19

God's grace that can save everyone has come. (Titus 2:11 NCV)

December 20

It's important to know that grace is enough for you to be deemed perfect, regardless of your church identity, stylistic preference, or personal holiness (only Christ was perfectly holy in the flesh). And to prevent elitist factions within Christianity, it's equally important to understand that grace is enough for everyone else, too, without regard to *their* church identity, stylistic preference, or personal holiness.

December 21

If it's difficult for you to accept any change around you, then it will be difficult for you to accept the Spirit's changes inside you.

December 22

> All a person's ways seem pure to them, but motives are weighed by the Lord. Commit to the Lord whatever you do, and he will establish your plans. The Lord works out everything. (Proverbs 16:2–4)

December 23

Waiting on God to work things out for you takes faith. Faith that your patience will pay off in the end. Faith that God is always faithful and won't disappoint you.

December 24

> We can make our plans, but the Lord determines our steps. (Proverbs 16:9 NLT)

❦

December 25

Patience could be the most important virtue to learn in life. You have to be willing to let things develop. If you try to force everything, your life will be in constant disarray.

December 26

> We do not make requests of (God) because we are righteous, but because of (His) great mercy. (Daniel 9:18)

❧❦❧

December 27

As faith matures, we stop inflexibly trying to steer God toward what we want (especially how and when we want it!). We obviously hope and pray for certain things—in fact, we pray *hard* for those things—but not for the purpose of getting our way. Prayer does so much good on so many levels; there's not enough space in this book to discuss all the purposes and benefits of prayer, but I can assure you that controlling the world is not one of them! In fact, it's quite the opposite. Prayer teaches us to trust God and get into alignment with His Spirit. We pray because we believe in God and we love Him, and we know that He loves us and wants to bless us. Eventually, we learn that it's not what we pray for that really matters; it's that we trust God enough to pray to Him from the bottom of our hearts. And when we pour our hearts out to God, things begin to happen; not the least of which is that we start to grow into the person that God wants us to be and has designs to use.

December 28

What begins as a passion for God will become a purpose for you.

❧

December 29

No one has ever imagined what God has prepared for those who love him. (1 Corinthians 2:9 NCV)

If we believe—and are gratefully aware—that God has our best interests at heart, then our prayers give us the peace that passes understanding (Philippians 4:6–7). God works things out for His glory, and our prayers should remind us that we are part of that glory and have nothing to fear. Romans 8:28 promises that *all things* work for the good of those who love God and are called according to *His purpose.* The mature element of that verse is to recognize that God's purpose is Jesus (Ephesians 1:9–10; Colossians 2:2); *so if Christ is also your purpose,* then you can rest assured that your life and your prayers will be used for the benefit of many (including you) and for the glory of the Lord!

December 31

The eyes of the Lord range throughout the earth to strengthen those whose hearts are fully committed to him. (2 Chronicles 16:9)

Printed in the United States
By Bookmasters